Offbeat BRISTOL

JAMES BELSEY

D1132173

REDCLIFFE
Bristol

First published in 1992 by
Redcliffe Press Ltd
49 Park St, Bristol.

ISBN 1 872971 22 9

British Library Cataloguing-in-Publication Data.
A catalogue record for this book is available
from the British Library.

Typeset and printed by
The Longdunn Press Ltd, Bristol

Contents

Credits

All the photographs in this book were taken by the author with
the exception of those on pages 7, 8, 11, 12, 15, 18, 21, 31, 43, 45
49, 59, 61, 62.

page 45: The Marriage of the Arnolfini by Jan van Eyck was
reproduced by courtesy of the Trustees, the National Gallery,
London.
page 15: Princess Caraboo by Edward Bird was reproduced by
courtesy of The City of Bristol Museum and Art Gallery.

Robinson Crusoe in Bristol

The early 18th century Bristol sea dog Captain Woodes Rogers made an astonishing discovery when he and his crew landed on an exotic South Seas island when escaping from a storm.

A bizarre figure stumbled towards them . . . a deeply tanned white man dressed in goatskins who brokenly explained how he had been a prisoner on the island for four years.

Gradually the story emerged. This strange person was a Scot, Alexander Selkirk, who had been marooned on his desert island after a shipboard dispute.

Luckily for him, the island offered shelter, water and plenty of nourishing food in the form of fish, wild goats, fruit and vegetables. Woodes Rogers took his exotic find on board and brought Selkirk safely back to the City Docks in Bristol and his home in Queen Square (a plaque at 33–35 marks the site). Selkirk lived in Bristol for some years, where he became first a local then a national celebrity.

His romantic tale of life marooned on a tropical island inspired Daniel Defoe's classic *Robinson Crusoe*.

It has been claimed that Defoe met Selkirk in Bristol and heard the story first-hand before writing the book but that's a fanciful myth.

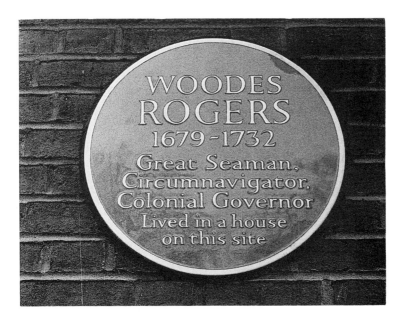

The fatal fall of the daredevil barber

Of all Bristol's daredevils, Charlie Stephens, the fearless barber of West Street, Bedminster was the greatest – and he died the most spectacular death possible in a stupendous act of courage.

Charlie's colourful career as a self-confessed 'tempter of fate' included shaving people in a lion's cage at the Bristol Coliseum, having an apple balanced on his throat sliced in two by a sword, parachuting in a red coat from balloons with landings on Chessel Street and Bedminster railway station, diving off the Forth Bridge and standing stock-still while crack shots knocked sugar cubes from the top of his scalp.

But they were mere aperitifs to the Big One. Charlie was determined to pull off the greatest stunt of all. He was going to ride the Niagara Falls in a barrel.

He had his barrel made in Bristol. It was painted in bright zebra stripes and specially cushioned for the gigantic forces of the world's most famous waterfall.

Charlie was convinced he could make his fortune from the film rights to his spectacular success in shooting the Falls and he was sealed into his barrel on July 11, 1920. Minutes later he was dead, his barrel smashed to smithereens and his body in pieces. All they found of this brave, likeable man was a severed arm which was interred in an unmarked grave in the local cemetery. The camera crew's fee was just £20, enough to cover the funeral expenses.

Charlie was 58. He left 11 children, a widow, Annie and an enduring memory as a larger-than-life character.

The slave Bristol remembers

At least one black slave who was a victim of the notorious transatlantic trade in humans does have a memorial in Bristol . . . the teenager Scipio Africanus.

Scipio lies buried in Henbury churchyard where his grave has long been an object of curiosity and pilgrimage.

There is an enduring myth that Bristol slavers brought their wretched cargoes of terrified Africans home to the City Docks and kept them in chains in Redcliffe caves before transporting them across the Atlantic.

In fact they were shipped directly from Africa to the colonies in the New World, part of the triangular trade in which merchants exchanged British goods for slaves on the West Coast of Africa and then slaves for produce like sugar and tobacco on the other side of the ocean.

But a small number of black men and women slaves did reach Britain, often becoming servants of rich folk looking for an exotic novelty to show off to guests. Scipio Africanus was one of them.

He was servant to the seventh Earl of Suffolk who lived in the now-demolished Great House near Henbury church. Scipio became much loved by the young Earl and his wife who treated him almost like a son.

The lad was just 18 when he died in 1720.

His memorial stone reads:

> I who was born a Pagan and a Slave,
> Now sleep sweetly a Christian in my grave,
> What tho' my hue was dark, my Saviour's sight

8

Mr Brunel's gateway to the world

Brunel House at the back of the Council House behind College Green hardly looks like the Gateway To The New World.

But that was how the brilliant engineer and pioneer Isambard Kingdom Brunel dreamt of his handsome building with its imposing facade.

It was named the Great Western Steamship Hotel when it opened in 1839 and it was designed as a luxurious resting place where rich voyagers would be pampered on their final night in England.

Brunel was a visionary who never did things by halves. His brilliantly successful Great Western Railway between London and Bristol was only part of a much, much more ambitious route . . . nothing less than the great journey from London to New York and then beyond.

The plan was thus: passengers would be whisked down to Bristol on the comfortable, broad gauge railway where they would spend the night at the Great Western Steamship Hotel.

From there it would be a brief journey by road to Severnside and the speed, excitement and comfort of Mr Brunel's latest transatlantic ocean liner . . . and then the great crossing.

Alas, the scheme was a flop, the transatlantic trade was lost to rival ports and the former hotel saw several changes of use. It was a Turkish bath, then an untidy hotch-potch of offices. It lay derelict for a while until the 1980s and a successful rescue plan which saved the historic facade and developed a modern office complex on the site.

The building is now the home of several Bristol City Council departments.

The wickedest pirate of them all

Bristol can boast a terrible rogues' gallery of reckless, vicious pirates . . . but none of them approach the devilry of the infamous Blackbeard.

This bizarre character was portrayed with relish by the star Robert Newton in the title role of the Hollywood film, but even Newton at his over-the-top best couldn't have matched the original.

Blackbeard hailed from Redcliffe and his real name was Edward or Edmund Teach. It was said he was responsible for more than 2,000 deaths during his reign of fear as the most bloodthirsty of all pirates in the early 18th century.

Teach specialised in horror tactics. He wore a long black beard and during assaults on ships he thrust smoking fuses into his beard and matted hair so that he hove into view like Satan himself, with a shawl of devil-like black smoke around his face.

Teach's favourite hunting ground was off the American coast and the West Indies where he terrorised shipping and won an appalling reputation for his "most bloody disposition . . . cruel to barbarity".

He is said to have married a dozen women bigamously before he met a fittingly violent death on the coast of Carolina, murdered by pirate-hunters.

The man who invented the blanket

Did a Bristolian invent the blanket? Yes, the legend goes. Not only invented but also gave the world's pre-duvet sleepers the name of their favourite winter bed-time warmer.

He was Ted Blanket who lived in the Temple district of the city in the 14th century when the area, near the present day Temple Meads station, was an important weaving centre.

One bitterly cold night in 1343 Ted ran out of firewood, his home was freezing so he took some soft, unfinished, loosely woven woollen cloth which he had brought home to experiment with, and laid it on his bed. Despite the freezing temperatures, he and Mrs Blanket had a remarkably warm night's sleep.

News of this new-fangled invention travelled fast and folk queued up to buy the very latest in household aids.

It's said that no less a person than King Edward III ordered two of Mr Blanket's remarkable woollen novelties, and that at that point Ted's fortune was made.

Fact or fiction? There WAS a notable weaver in Temple called Ted Blanket, he did make a fortune and he did become a bailiff of the city and a Member of Parliament.

Ted lies buried in St Stephen's Church, just off the city centre. Wrapped in a blanket? Perhaps.

Alfred, King of Bristol Zoo

Alfred the Gorilla was more than just one of the most prized exhibits at Bristol Zoo . . . he was a celebrity.

The lowland gorilla arrived in Clifton as a two-and-a-half to three-year-old furry toddler on September 5, 1930 and he was an instant hit.

During those early years little Alfred was a familiar sight in his collar and chain being taken for walkies by his keeper. But the good life at the zoo saw him putting on height and weight, and before long Alfred was too big and powerful to ramble at a chain's length and he was caged in an increasingly secure gorilla house.

Alfred loved children and adored playing hide and seek with youngsters by running in and out of the inner cage in his compound.

When Alfred died in 1948, Bristolians couldn't bear to part with their old friend from the zoo. He represented too many memories. So they had Alfred stuffed and put him back on show, this time at the City Museum in Queen's Road where you can see him to this day.

But there is a memento at the zoo itself, a sculpted bust of his head which pays tribute to a very popular character.

Mr Millions and his Bedminster hoop-la stall

Billy Butlin paid just £1.50 in Lock's Yard, Bedminster for a hoop-la stall in a travelling fair . . . and a multi-million pound fortune was launched.

Born in South Africa in 1899, he came to live in Bristol as a little boy when his mum married a Bristol gas worker. He went to St Mary Redcliffe School for a while before emigrating to Canada.

After World War I service with the Canadian army, he worked his passage across the Atlantic to Liverpool, was paid £5 and walked 160 miles back to Bristol to join the Marshall Hill fair at its Bedminster winter base.

Billy made his hoop-la pedestals the easiest to 'hoop', gave out prizes more quickly than anyone . . . and took 10 times the profits of his stunned rivals with their penny-pinching attractions as he triumphantly toured the West Country on the travelling fair circuit.

He went from hoop-la stalls to amusement parks to zoos and, in 1935, to his first holiday camp in Skegness, an idea he'd long since dreamed about after remembering a rotten holiday on the Bristol Channel when he'd been thrown out of his lodgings by a seaside landlady who wouldn't allow 'guests' to stay during the day.

Give the punters a fair deal, a roof over their heads and amusements, and they would flock in just as they had to his Bedminster hoop-la stall. And, of course, it worked.

Her hoaxing Highness . . . Princess Caraboo

She was the prettiest exotic princess Bristol had ever seen . . . and the cleverest hoaxer of them all.

She was "Princess Caraboo", a beautiful, dark creature who arrived mysteriously in Almondsbury in April, 1815. She caused a sensation. Her hair was swathed in a turban of scarves, she spoke a strange, babbling language no-one could understand but by gesture she explained that she was an important person – and that she was in desperate trouble from her enemies.

Little by little her tale unfolded. She revealed that she was none other than Princess Caraboo from the distant land of Javanu where she had been kidnapped by merciless pirates.

But fate had come to her aid when the pirate ship sailed up the Bristol Channel. She had seized her chance by jumping overboard and swimming to the shore near Aust.

The self-styled Princess fooled everyone, including Bristol's Town Clerk who gave her a home and revelled in his celebrity guest.

Princess Caraboo was fêted as Bristol's most fascinating personage for more than two months and her fame spread across the country. She even gave oriental sword-fighting displays to demonstrate the wonders of Javanu's martial arts 'traditions'. That, perhaps, was painting the lily.

Because shortly afterwards, Her Royal Highness was rumbled. She was, in fact, plain Mary Baker, a cobbler's daughter from Devon. Mary had hoodwinked thousands, from rich merchants and aristocrats to the most humble.

Mary was hurried off to America to spare everyone's blushes and in a vain hope that the tale of Princess Caraboo would be quietly forgotten. It wasn't, of course.

But years later Mary did return under her own name and she lies buried in Arno's Vale cemetery in Bristol, the city she so cleverly duped.

Princess Caraboo painted by Edward Bird, 1817

Bristol's Beatles world-beater

One Beatles' worldwide smash hit was inspired by a stroll around Bristol's city centre, and one of the loveliest of their songs at that.

Paul McCartney was in Bristol in November, 1965 to join his 19-year-old actress girlfriend Jane Asher who was appearing in the title role of a new play *Cleo* by Frank Marcus at the Bristol Old Vic's Theatre Royal in King Street and breaking box office records.

Paul popped down to Bristol from time to time during the play's run. One evening while Jane was on stage at the Theatre Royal he went for a walk through the nearby streets, his face disguised by a scarf and hat. Beatlemania was still at its height and he would have been mobbed if he'd been recognised.

A theme had been buzzing in his head about a girl called Daisy Hawkins, but the name somehow wouldn't fit with the tune he'd been tinkering with alongside his collaborator John Lennon.

Daisy, Daisy . . . perhaps Eleanor instead? And then Paul glanced at a shop on the city centre, saw the shopkeeper's name of Rigby and everything fell into place. The result was one of pop music's finest classics.

The cat and the cook

It isn't just the famous and the noble who are buried at Bristol's stately St Mary Redcliffe Church, the one a delighted Queen Elizabeth I described as "the fairest, goodliest and most famous parish church in England" on her visit in 1574.

An excellent chef and a friendly cat have their resting places there, too.

The cook was William Coke, chef to the great 15th century Bristol merchant William Canynges. The chef was so highly regarded that he has his own grave slab in the church's south transept complete with the insignia of his art . . . a colander and a knife.

The moggy was a black pussy known simply as the Church Cat who turned up as a kitten in 1912, lived in the church thereafter and showed a great love for organ music, always sitting on the organist's knee whenever he was playing. She has her little tombstone in the churchyard which simply reads: The Church Cat 1912-1927.

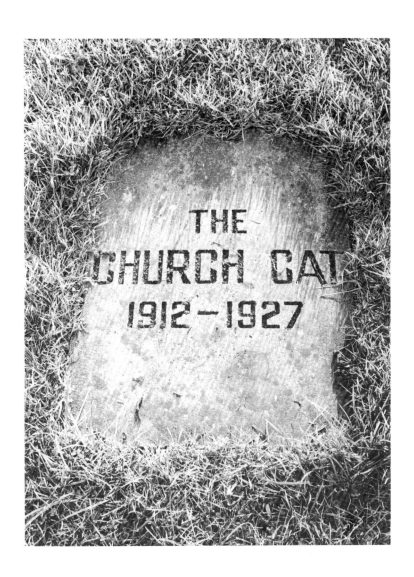

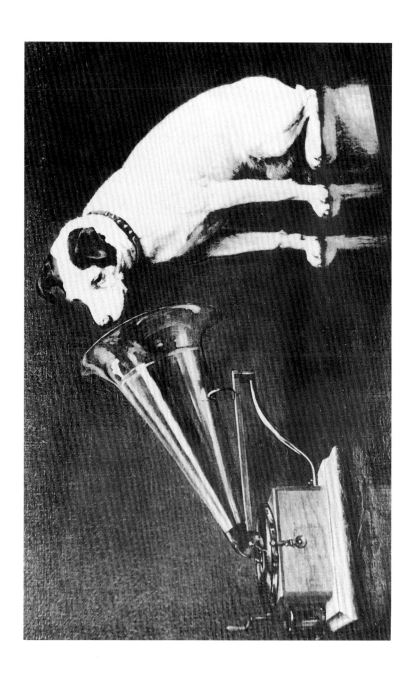

Nipper . . . still listening for His Master's Voice

When lists are drawn up of Bristol's best-known Victorian characters, they always seem to forget Nipper. But Nipper's probably the most famous of them all, a figure known across the world.

He was a mongrel with a touch of bull terrier and a century later he's still celebrated for his role as that loyal pooch listening to His Master's Voice.

The Bristol-born dog was bought as a pup in 1884 by flamboyant Bristol theatrical artist Mark Barraud and the two became inseparable. When some of Mark's most brilliant sets for exotic shows at the Prince's Theatre in Park Row won a standing ovation, Nipper would join his master on stage for a bow.

When Barraud died in 1887, leaving a widow and five children, his brother Francis gave Nipper a home and the dog became fascinated by the family's phonograph. He would sit quietly listening to the horn loudspeaker, ears cocked.

Nipper and his second master later moved to Kingston-on-Thames where the dog died in 1895 and was buried under a mulberry tree in the garden. Three years later Francis painted his immortal picture in memory of a dearly-loved pal.

The original painting was sold to the Gramophone Company for £100 and in 1908 Nipper replaced the company's original logo . . . so becoming one of the most famous pets of all.

By 1950 Nipper was such a superstar that the record company HMV, named after the picture, wanted to remove his remains to their headquarters in Hayes.

Alas, Nipper's bones had been covered by a newly-built concrete car park. And there he rests.

Exit Archie Leach . . . enter Cary Grant

Cary Grant will never be superseded as Bristol's most glamorous 20th century son . . . but Archie Leach, his real name, certainly left his native city under a cloud.

The stage-struck lad was a pupil at Fairfield Grammar School in Montpelier and he spent every spare moment hanging around Bristol's theatres, hoping for a break into show business.

At last his chance came with an opportunity to join a knockabout act of boy comedians run by the clown Bob Pender. Archie ran away from home but was tracked down with the Pender boys 10 days later by his father and returned to Bristol and to Fairfield school.

It was war. Archie was determined to re-join Pender so he became the baddest boy in Fairfield, skipping classes and then, finally, sneaking across to the school's girls section with a mate and accepting a dare to enter the girls' loos. He was grabbed by a burly hockey teacher and, the next morning, publicly expelled in front of the assembled school. Three days later he re-joined the Pender troupe.

Which perhaps explains why, for the rest of his life, Cary Grant wryly inserted an inaccurate line in *Who's Who* about his education. His school, the entry stated, was one Fairfield Academy in Somerset.

The £1 million-a-day bicycle ride

Every day of the working week he'd arrive promptly on his bicycle at 3.30 p.m., a cheque for £1 million or so tucked safely away in his pocket.

His daily ride took him across Bedminster Bridge on the short journey from W.D. and H.O. Wills' redbrick factory and offices in East Street to the Custom House in Queen Square.

This bicycling millionaire wasn't famous, just a duty clerk in the tobacco giant's finance department who was glad to get out of the office and enjoy a little fresh air and exercise on the interesting journey past St Mary Redcliffe Church and the east end of the City Docks, its quaysides busy with dockers unloading ships.

The cheque he carried was Wills' payment for the next day's duty on the raw tobacco leaf taken out of the bonded warehouses at the Ashton end of the City Docks.

No more. Wills left for Hartcliffe and first its name and then cigarette production vanished from Bristol. The Customs left their Queen Square home. And, anyway, computers have replaced that bicycle in fast-forwarding payments.

20

Saved – the Three Lamps

Bristol thought it had lost its lovely old Three Lamps sign at the junction of the Bath and Wells roads when Totterdown was demolished to make way for an urban motorway which was never built.

The acres cleared for that planned road are now buried by new housing estates and Totterdown is a residential district once more.

And the eye-catching Three Lamps sign is back again after a lengthy spell spent at the City Engineer's depot in Ashley Down, just by the main railway line to the Midlands. Passengers leaving Bristol for Birmingham and points north could see it clearly.

The sign was well worth saving. It's one of the best surviving early 19th century road signs in Britain and Bristol has done it proud, lovingly restoring the handsome letterwork and cast iron column and creating a fittingly attractive surround of brickwork and railings now that the Three Lamps stands once more on the spot it originally occupied.

Lloyd-Webber's Bristol nightmare . . . and triumph

Andrew Lloyd-Webber's career as a talented young composer of musicals was on the rocks when his brand new show *Jeeves*, co-written with Tim Rice, was given a pre-London run at the Bristol Hippodrome.

The musical, based on the immortal P.G. Wodehouse character, was clearly doomed to be a disaster and a despairing Lloyd-Webber, who seemed to have the Midas touch after brilliant successes with both *Joseph And His Technicolour Dreamcoat* and *Jesus Christ Superstar*, saw his reputation about to go up in the flames.

He left a particularly dreadful performance at the Hippodrome in despair, walking across the Centre to the Unicorn Hotel where he locked himself into his room, put all thoughts of rescuing his Jeeves musical behind him and wrote an agonised first number for a new musical light years away from the Wodehousian world of toffs, butlers and country house weekends.

The song? 'Don't Cry For Me Argentina', the cornerstone of the daring musical *Evita* based on the life of Eva Peron, glitzy wife of a South American dictator. It was to be the number which, above all others, confirmed Lloyd-Webber as one of the most popular stage composers of the 20th century.

The sinister Castle of Arno's Vale

The Black Castle at Arno's Vale just off the Bath Road is a thoroughly sinister-looking place . . . it doesn't take much imagination to think of prisoners locked in dungeons, dark secrets and satanic rites.

Little wonder, then, that as the writer Horace Wapole arrived in Brislington in 1766 on a journey to Bristol he was taken aback by the "large Gothic building, coal black and striped with white. I took it for the Devil's Cathedral!"

In fact the Black Castle is a weird and wonderful folly built in the shape of a castle by wealthy copper smelter William Reeve to house offices and stables opposite his home Mount Pleasant, now the Arno's Court Hotel.

And that blackness comes from the very unusual building materials which Reeves used. The walls are made of black copper-slag blocks recycled from his works at Crew's Hole.

The lordly lions

The noble lions of Cambridge Park in Redland are so imposing that most people think they must mark the entrance to a long-lost mansion.

Not so. North west Bristol's most popular pair of statues are there to mark the icing on the cake of a handsome and successful piece of Victorian property development.

Cambridge Park was built in the mid-19th century as a genteel, exclusive cul-de-sac. A smart pair of stone pillars were erected at the entrance.

The lions came later, a final flourish after all the new homes had been sold. They are almost certainly copies of the statues at Lion Lodge at Piercefield Park in the Wye Valley.

Cambridge Park's lions could well have been lost in 1958 when a lorry crashed into the pillars, sending both statues toppling. One was badly damaged, the other scarred.

But local people campaigned so vociferously for the lions to be repaired and restored that stonemasons were called in, the statues lovingly mended and the Cambridge Park's great cats took their rightful place once more.

The flying tramline

There it stands, Bristol's oddest war memento but one which still has the power to make Blitz veterans shudder.

It is a hefty tram rail which, like some bizarre Excalibur, lies embedded hilt-deep in the graveyard of St Mary Redcliffe Church. It has been there since a high explosive German bomb ripped apart the nearby roads and sent this horrifyingly murderous hunk of metal cannoning through the night air.

Mercifully, it impaled nothing more than the turf in the last of the great Bristol blitzes, the Good Friday raid of April 11, 1941.

And, equally mercifully, the beautiful church itself escaped damage that night just as it had done in the previous five major raids which had laid waste to so many nearby buildings.

The girder was violently uprooted from the tramline junction of Redcliffe Hill and Guinea Street, was such a vivid reminder of the violence of those dreadful nights of the winter and spring of 1940/41 that the church authorities decided to leave it where it had landed.

Today it's an object of curiosity, almost amusement to the young.

Older folk who lived through those nights still find it a chilling sight.

Royal York Crescent's most regal home

It's easily the prettiest house in Royal York Crescent with its pillars and lofty entrance . . . and it has the prettiest name of any house in Bristol. Eugenie.

The name is beautifully displayed on the front of Number 2, Royal York Crescent and it commemmorates a very special resident.

She was little Eugenie, later to become the Empress Eugenie of France and wife of Napoleon III, who came to Bristol to study at a fashionable school at Number 2.

That name isn't the only curiosity in Royal York Crescent. Walk along a little and you'll notice that there is no Number 13. There's a house between numbers 12 and 14 . . . but it has a compromise number for a superstitious owner. It's called 12A.

Pitch and Pay Lane

Pitch and Pay Lane. It sounds such a jolly, cheerful name reminiscent of children's games, larks and fun . . . but its true story is a sad, sinister one.

The lane was once a little country road centuries before this part of modern Bristol had been developed by rich Victorians into the smart suburb of Stoke Bishop.

That odd name recalls dark days when the old city of Bristol was often struck by plagues and epidemics. The City Docks were notoriously filthy and contagious diseases were one of the sorrier results of living beside what was nothing less than an open sewer.

Bristol's reputation for disease was so bad that country folk living around the town were always on the alert for some fresh danger to their health. When some new outbreak did occur, Gloucestershire farmers and smallholders refused to come near the place. They were only prepared to sell their produce at a safe distance from the unhealthy citizens.

So, at this pre-arranged spot, they developed the practice of pitching their produce at the waiting, hungry Bristolians . . . while the citizens paid by throwing back the necessary cash. It was an early example of the quarantine principle – pitching, paying and preventing the spread of illness.

The all-seeing Observatory

Clifton Observatory is one of Bristol's oddest-looking buildings and its position is even odder, standing in stark isolation on the highest spot in Bristol on the site of an ancient British camp just above the Clifton Suspension Bridge. You can still see the outlines of the hillfort's ramparts more than 2,000 years later.

This odd, tower-like structure was, in fact, a windmill, strategically placed to take advantage of the prevailing south-westerly winds and it did its job well until mighty winds sent the sails flying so quickly that the friction caused the mechanism to burst into flames, setting fire to the mill.

William West, an entrepreneurial artist with a romantic eye, turned the attractive ruin into an Observatory half a century later, installing powerful telescopes and the famous Camera Obscura which is still a tourist attraction today. The Camera swings to project a 360 degree picture of Bristol on to a circular screen in a darkened room at the top of the building.

West developed his lucrative side-show by excavating a passage to the subterranean Giant Ghyston's cave, installing a Gorge-side viewpoint for visitors where the cave opens to the sheer rock face.

29

Thomas Goldney's cave of jewels

Aladdin's cave was said to sparkle with a million jewels . . . and so does the cave that Thomas Goldney created in the lavish gardens of his hillside home in Clifton.

Goldney was a rich merchant who sent his ships to some of the world's most exotic places. Their orders were to bring home the most profitable items from across the oceans – and to collect shells, sparkling stones, coral and other bright and shiny pieces for the grotto he began to build in 1737.

Thomas Goldney's grotto took nearly 30 years to complete. He was delighted with the result and his delight has been shared by generations of romantics ever since. The cave is a fairyland of glints, lights and sparkles and one of the most brilliant follies in the world.

Today Goldney's home and garden belong to Bristol University. Goldney House is a student hall of residence. But the garden is open to the public from time to time . . . and so is Mr Goldney's fabulous cave.

Fountain on the move

Old Thomas Proctor's fountain is one of Bristol's most fanciful – and weighty – Victorian monuments . . . but that didn't stop it from hitching up its masonry skirts and crossing one of the city's busier roads.

Alderman Thomas Proctor had the drinking fountain built at the top of Bridge Valley Road in 1872 on the site of the old Clifton turnpike. But by the end of the 1980s, it had become a traffic hazard hiding the view of cars approaching this busy junction from the Portway.

So the fountain was moved stone by stone and feature by feature . . . across the main road to the green by the Mansion House.

Alderman Proctor made another handsome gift to Bristol. Using the name Nil Desperandum (never despair) he secretly donated the first cash to restore St Mary Redcliffe Church. The fountain is designed by London architect George Godwin, who began that St Mary Redcliffe restoration.

Bristol's most crowded bomb shelter – the Portway Tunnel

Today it stands locked and derelict, its entrance half hidden by thick undergrowth.

But during the worst of the Bristol blitzes in the winter of 1940/41, people would walk for miles to find shelter in the tunnel that lies beneath Bridge Valley Road in the shadow of the Clifton Suspension Bridge.

The tunnel gained a near-mythical reputation as the safest place to be when bombs were falling over Bristol, and families shoved and squeezed their way into the dank, unhealthy interior to pass the night.

So many began traipsing to the tunnel each night that the authorities acted, fearing riots or, worse, an epidemic from the increasingly filthy conditions in the tunnel. Hundreds of people were forcibly evicted from the Portway refuge and ordered not to return. A small number of treasured passes were issued to the lucky few.

The action caused bitter resentment among a hungry, blitz-weary population. But as the fear of blitzes began to die away after the final great raids of the spring of 1941 faded, so did the ill-feeling.

The Palace at the end of the line

Old Market regulars call in the Gin Palace because that's just what it looks like.

But the Palace, that wildly grandiose, oddly out-of-place pub at the east end of Old Market had a grander purpose when it was built in the 1860s.

The railways were already very big business and with them came success for the smart hotels built at the end of every busy line. Speculative entrepreneurs were convinced that an important railway station was destined for Old Market . . . and so up went the Palace, ready and waiting for all the passengers who would make the speculators' fortunes.

It never happened.

Temple Meads was expanded from the original Bristol and Exeter station and although a terminus for the Midland line was built at nearby St Philips, it wasn't near enough to save the Palace. The great hotel was stranded, its purpose unfulfilled and it was converted into a pub.

Aaargh . . . Jim Lad!

There's only one thing certain about that famous fictional meeting between the piratical Long John Silver and young Jim Hawkins, Jim Lad of *Treasure Island* fame.

That it took place in Bristol.

"I go to Bristol" is the title of the chapter and our Jim meets the wicked old boy in a dockside pub called, tantalisingly, the Spyglass.

So which pub was Stevenson thinking of when he wrote Treasure Island? Some claim it was the Llandoger Trow in King Street. Unlikely. A far better bet would appear to be the nearby Hole In The Wall on the corner of Redcliffe Way and the Grove.

The Hole In The Wall really does have a spy glass in front of the building which would have offered a good view of any approaching gang hoping to hunt down young men for forcible or 'pressed' service at sea and it stands only yards from the Grove, once one of the busiest of the famous Bristol quaysides.

The Hole In The Wall seems to fit the bill very well!

35

The Rummer

The Rummer . . . it's a good name for one of Bristol's most famous and ancient inns.

Rummer. The name smacks of curiosity as in 'rummy', of hard liquor as in rum and lots of activity.

True in every case when it comes to this lovely old pub, except that the real answer to the puzzle of the name can be found near the old staircase designed by the architect John Wood when he rebuilt the tavern in the mid-18th century as part of the area's redevelopment when his magnificent Corn Exchange was taking shape a stone's throw away.

A rummer is a large drinking mug for rum and the Rummer displays a fine example of one of these vessels, made of copper and wood. Visitors in these health-conscious days boggle at the rummer's capacity.

Why paint a tree white?

That's a question most Bristolians, let alone visitors, ask when they drive north across the Downs and around White Tree roundabout with its young tree resplendent with its waistcoat of paint.

The littl'un you see today is the third White Tree to stand near this spot. The first, a tall, mature specimen had to be removed in 1951 as part of a traffic scheme when the roundabout was built not long after World War II. A nearby elm was chosen as White Tree mark 2, but it died in the Dutch Elm Disease epidemic of the 1970s.

Today's is a young lime which was planted in 1975 and it's given a fresh coat of paint once a year.

No-one really knows how this curious tradition began in the mid-19th century, but there are several theories. One says it was painted white to guide a German tutor across the Downs to Cote House, where he taught the family's children. A second claims it was painted by a well-known host to guide his friends from town to his house and table in Etloe Road.

Or perhaps, as a third tale goes, it acted as a signpost to a local coachman with a rotten sense of direction and an over-liking for the pubs of Clifton. It showed him the way to totter home!

But the likeliest theory is that the White Tree is no more than a convenient road sign which marked the northern exit from the Downs for coachmen in the pre-tarmac days.

The miracle fall

The luckiest children alive . . . those were little Elsie Brown and her 12-year-old sister Ruby who survived a spectacular murder attempt by their father on the Clifton Suspension Bridge in September, 1896.

Charles Brown, a Birmingham grocer, was bankrupt and losing his mind. He had five children and could no longer support his family. In despair he took the two girls all the way to Bristol and to the Suspension Bridge.

The wretched children were forced to walk up and down in the darkness, howling winds and pouring rain for an hour until their maddened father suddenly seized first Ruby and then Elsie and hurled them over the parapet.

The girls' guardian angels must have been on overtime that dreadful night.

For the winds were so violent that great upcurrents of air somehow caught the falling bodies and cushioned their falls.

And a further chance in a million. The girls both splashed into the murky waters of the River Avon within a few feet of a passing pilot boat. It was the work of a moment to drag the terrified youngsters to safety.

Both Elsie and Ruby suffered nasty bruises and injuries and were kept in hospital. But both were back on their feet within days.

The Avon Gorge Zig Zag

It's an exciting journey on foot on the way down with some of the most spectacular views in the West Country . . . and a puff and a pant on the way back! That's the aptly named Zig Zag in the Avon Gorge.

This dramatic path zigs and zags its way down from a point opposite the St Vincent's Rock Hotel on Sion Hill to Hotwells and the Portway more than 200 feet below and, some claim, it has its very own Royal patron.

For there is an enduring tale that Princess Victoria used to play on the path when she was a little girl, before her accession to the throne as a teenager in 1837, and that she pointed out her childhood haunt to Prince Albert when they visited Bristol to launch the s.s. *Great Britain* on July 19, 1843.

Edward Everard's palace

You could live in Bristol all your life and still miss the secret palace that Edward Everard the printer built himself in Broad Street.

With its fairy-tale towers, jewel-like colours and heroic figures of craftsmen/printers of two ages, Everard's palace is one of Britain's most brilliant arts and crafts movement buildings and one of Bristol's greatest decorative treasures. If you can find it, of course.

Everard's stands so far back from Broad Street that there's not a hint of the place until you're standing smack in front of it.

Then you can enjoy the dazzling Doulton tiled facade with its winged Spirit of Literature, its portraits of the early printer Gutenburg and the 19th century arts and crafts master William Morris and its mass of decorative details.

Everard's was built as a printing works which ran from Broad Street to Little John Street behind. Today the sound of the presses has been replaced by the hum-and-tack of computers and hi-tech keyboards. Everard's secret palace has become part of a banking office complex.

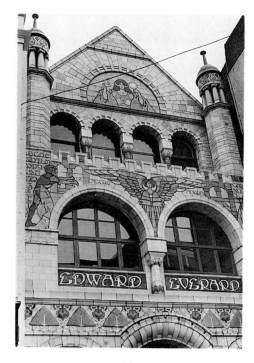

The hottest restaurant in town

Newcomers who eat at Bristol's smart Kiln restaurant between Temple Meads station and St Mary Redcliffe Church are rarely aware that they're eating in what was once one of the hottest places in old Bristol.

For the Kiln is the sole survivor of more than a dozen conical glassworks which stood in what was once one of the West Country's busiest industrial areas. They looked like huge, pointed beehives and they belched smoke, giving newcomers arriving from London along the great West road an alarming welcome to the city.

Until 1930 the last remaining kiln stood at an impressive 150 feet until the upper sections were demolished, leaving the remains we know today.

For years that odd-looking, circular building was lost to view, hidden by tall billboards until it was dramatically revealed in the 1970s as part of the development of the adjoining Dragonara, now Hilton hotel.

It was too good an oddity not to save . . . so this fascinating relic of Bristol's industrial past was converted into one of the most striking and unusual-looking restaurants in Europe.

Bristol's
leaning tower

Pisa has its famous leaning tower – and so does Bristol with its drunkenly off-vertical tower of Temple Church in Temple Street.

The tower isn't on the stupendous scale of its Italian counterpart, it's true.

But its prominent position by busy Victoria Street and its proximity to Temple Meads station make it one of the most startling sights to be seen by newly-arrived visitors to Bristol.

Poor old Temple Church was badly blitzed during the air raids of World War II and the building remains a gutted ruin half a century later.

But it wasn't enemy bombs which caused the tower to reel over five foot out of true. That happened after it was rebuilt in 1460. The foundations caused problems which couldn't be solved, the tower began to move but, at last, it settled at today's offbeat angle.

There has been a church on this site since 1145 when the mysterious order of Knights Templar erected their chapel here – nearby Temple Meads takes its name from the order.

A little piece of Bristol in a foreign land

Well, quite a large piece of old Bristol and it lies buried 3,000 miles across the Atlantic beneath East River Drive in New York City.

It is tons of rubble from buildings wrecked in the Bristol Blitzes of World War II which was ferried across the Atlantic in war-time by American Liberty ships.

These vessels brought desperately-needed goods to the people of Britain via Avonmouth docks, but once their cargoes had been unloaded, they were dangerously unstable.

Without cargoes or heavy ballast, the ships could well have split at the seams or capsized on the rough crossing back to their East Coast harbours. The answer lay by the ton-load in areas of Bristol flattened by bombs.

Until then this rubble had been ferried into the Bristol Channel and dumped overboard. Now it had a more useful job to do helping American sailors to get safely home.

And the rubble didn't go to waste on the far side of the Atlantic. In New York City the great East River Drive highway was under construction and the ex-ballast was used as foundations for the motorway. A plaque was placed by the roadside to record the tale.

After the area was redeveloped for waterside apartments, the plaque was reinstated and unveiled in 1974 by the Bristol-born Hollywood film star Cary Grant. In a delightfully flamboyant gesture Cary arrived at the ceremony in a British double-decker bus.

43

Arnolfini who?

What's in a name? A bit of a mystery for many people when it comes to the Arnolfini, Bristol's famous modern art gallery housed on the two lower floors of the massive Bush warehouse on Narrow Quay.

Arnolfini? Who's he? Something to do with an Arnold someone-or-other? Not a bit of it.

Bristol's Arnolfini made its first appearance in 1960 when former art student and modern art enthusiast Jeremy Rees and some friends decided that the city needed its own modern gallery. But what to call it?

He remembered a favourite picture, Jan Van Eyck's *The Marriage of the Arnolfini* painted in 1434, one of the masterpieces of Dutch art. It is a portrait of an Italian merchant with his bride and it now hangs in the National Gallery in London.

The Bristol gallery needed an unusual, striking name . . . and Arnolfini was certainly that! The name stuck.

Bristol's Arnolfini had a nomadic early life. It originally opened in a large upstairs room in Triangle West, Clifton and then made a brief stay at a disused warehouse in Queen Square before arriving at another empty warehouse on Canon's Road. Then, at last, it found its permanent headquarters at the old tea warehouse on Narrow Quay where it has stayed ever since.

Among its many accolades, the Arnolfini was made the subject of a Royal Mail postage stamp as part of a series celebrating outstanding successes in restoring old industrial buildings.

The Marriage of the Arnolfini by Jan van Eyck hangs in the National Gallery, London

Pay up – on the nail

"Cash on the Nail" the man said . . . and a century or so ago in Bristol he really meant it.

For the deal would have been clinched on one of Bristol's four famous nails standing outside the Corn Exchange on Corn Street or, from the late 1550s to 1771, under a covered walk outside All Saints Church before they were moved to today's well-known site.

The brass nails with their flat tops and raised edges to prevent coins tumbling onto the pavement, were made as convenient tables for merchants to carry out their business . . . hence the expressions "nailing a deal" and cash on the nail.

The oldest pillar hasn't got a date but experts say it is late Elizabethan. The second was given by Bristol merchant Robert Kitchen, who died in 1594. The two remaining nails are dated 1625 and 1631.

Robert Kitchen's nail was slightly bent when it was struck by a lorry in 1963. The pillar is so heavy that a crane had to be used to lift it before it could be replaced securely. A large crowd gathered, worried that someone might be making off with an important part of Bristol's history.

The workmen quickly reassured them . . . and the nail was replaced the next day.

Neptune
on the move

Neptune stands at the head of St Augustine's Reach on the City Centre looking as if he had been there forever.

Far from it. Neptune must be Bristol's most travelled statue.

The old man of the sea was cast in lead and set up in 1723 in Temple Street when a new conduit or water pipe was made. He had his own fountain. He and his fountain were twice moved around Temple Street, but always within yards of Temple church with its famous leaning tower.

Then, in 1872, Neptune was settled at the junction of Victoria Street and Temple Street. He stayed there until 1949 when he was given his present site and a smart granite base at St Augustine's bridgehead.

The old boy even took a month long break from Bristol on one occasion. That was in the 1980s when experts realised that his lead bodywork needed attention.

So Neptune was carted off for a long-overdue service before resuming his rightful place as one of Bristol's best-loved street characters.

The Flying Cod

Bedminster's Flying Cod must be one of south Bristol's greatest street sign eye-catchers.

The hefty figure of a fish adorns the front of Webb's fresh fish shop in East Street, Bedminster, where it gazes across the road at the redeveloped site of the former tobacco giant Wills.

The fish swam into public view when it was erected in East Street in 1990 thanks to a government initiative to brighten up inner city areas and within months it had become one of the most talked-about and admired bits of street decoration.

Buses stop just outside the shop and the staff at Webb's love seeing the expressions on the faces of top deck passengers new to the route. They're goggle-eyed . . . or cod-eyed!

Boxkite feats

It hangs from the ceiling of the Bristol City Museum in Queen's Road, Clifton, a mad contraption of strings and wire . . . and one of the most significant engineering products ever made.

The *Bristol Boxkite* – called that because it looked just like one – was the brainchild of Sir George White, Bristol's tramways boss and the founder of the Bristol Aeroplane Company and the British aviation industry.

First he flew French aircraft at his Filton airfield and factory – then came the home-made *Bristol Boxkite*, unveiled dramatically with a public flying display on Durdham Down in 1910, piloted by a Frenchman.

The plane was so successful that before long, two were being made a week and the order book was full.

And its place in world history was assured within months of that dramatic lift-off. A *Bristol Boxkite* was fitted with a morse key and carried out aerial reconnaisance during autumn manoeuvres on Salisbury Plain.

It was the first time any aircraft had been flown for military purposes. A new age had begun.

Towering discoveries

The fanciful Cabot Tower on Brandon Hill is one of Bristol's most exotic landmarks.

The foundation stone was laid during a lavish ceremony on June 24, 1897, the 400th anniversary of John and Sebastian Cabot's discovery of mainland America aboard the Bristol ship the *Matthew*. Across the Atlantic in Halifax, Nova Scotia, there was a big ceremony too.

The tower was opened the following year, the work of Bristol architect William Venn Gough whose other buildings in Bristol include Colston's Girls School on Cheltenham Road and the former Port of Bristol Authority offices on Queen Square.

Cabot Tower stands 105 feet tall and is capped by a gilded, winged figure representing the spirit of commerce mounted on a globe of the world.

Did he dive or didn't he?

Only one person has claimed to have made the daredevil dive from the Clifton Suspension Bridge into the River Avon more than 250 foot below and survived - American adventurer Lawrence Donovan.

This noisy self-publicist arrived in Bristol in 1889. He told everyone who would listen to him that he had already dived from the Brooklyn Bridge in New York, half the height of its British counterpart, and that he was ready for Clifton's far greater challenge.

The day and time were announced and crowds gathered to watch his spectacular attempt.

Donovan made a great show of stomping back and forth along the bridge, but always with police alongside him. Whenever he made the slightest move to go near the edge, he was promptly restrained by the officers. After a while the crowds melted away, disappointed.

But one night shortly afterwards a carriage driven by two men came clattering onto the bridge. Out came a figure which plunged into the water below. Almost immediately afterwards Donovan was rescued on the Leigh Woods side of the river, claiming he had made his dive wearing a specially-designed metal body protector.

Onlookers say it was a dummy, not Donovan, which had sailed through the air and smashed into the water.

Donovan was taken to hospital at once. The sceptical staff who examined the remarkably unharmed American remarked dourly that the adventurer was suffering from "an ailment certainly not caused by a jump from the bridge".

The lover who leapt . . . and lived

Only a handful of people have survived the terrible fall from the Clifton Suspension Bridge. The most celebrated was young lover Sarah Ann Henley.

Sarah was a local girl from St Philip's in Bristol. In 1885 she was 22 and working in a Bristol factory when she was jilted by her boyfriend.

The heartbroken girl made her way up from industrial St Philips to Clifton and the bridge and, in despair, she leapt from the parapet. She was saved by Victorian women's fashion.

This was the age of wide skirts and voluminous petticoats and as she tumbled through the air, this mass of material acted like a sort of parachute to break her fall. Instead of crashing like a stone she drifted in the wind and sailed across to a sticky landing in the deep mud of the riverside.

The drama wasn't over. Her rescue from the mud was a difficult business but at last she was brought safely to firm ground and then to hospital where she was found, amazingly, to have suffered no more than a few light bruises but deep shock.

Sarah's tale has a happy ending. She later married, lived to the ripe old age of 84 and was quite a celebrity.

Bristol's laziest giant

There's a rocky mass in Blaise Woods which looks a little like an enormous armchair . . . it's called Giant Goram's Chair after one of a pair of monsters who lived on the Avon.

Goram, the tale goes, was the idle brother of the hard-working Vincent who spent his days hacking out the Avon Gorge with an enormous pick-axe.

Goram was supposed to be sharing the work with his brother. The arrangement was that at the end of each shift, they'd throw the pick-axe to each other with a warning yell.

But idle Goram took one post-lunch snooze too many on that fateful day. He'd long since settled comfortably into his rocky chair when Vincent's warning shout rang out.

The flying pick-axe hit him on the head and killed him instantly.

The Seven Sisters

They're called the Seven Sisters but in fact Bristol's best-known group of trees numbered half a dozen for many years . . . and then they were reduced to five.

This imposing group of mature pine trees is one of the most recognisable landmarks on Durdham Down, the northern half of Bristol's most famous open space, the Downs.

When the group was originally planted, they formed a loose circle with one tree in the centre. But the pine in the middle failed to mature, probably for lack of light and space as the other six prospered and grew taller by the year. It died and was removed.

The six remained a familiar sight for decades until the great January gale of 1990 when one fell victim to the mighty winds and was torn to the ground. Another lost one of its main branches but survived.

Afterwards two replacement pines were planted to re-create the original number – but this time they were planted outside the main circle to ensure a healthy future.

A giant tomb for a giant of a man

Ram Mohun Roy was a giant of a man in every sense, one of the 19th century's greatest reformers and a founding father of the world's largest democracy.

So when he died suddenly on a brief visit to Bristol, it was only fitting that he should be given Bristol's most exotic, magnificent memorial.

Today it is still the grandest of any to be found at Arno's Vale cemetery.

Roy's grave attracts pilgrims from many countries but especially from India, where he is revered as a founder of modern India and a leading reformer of his day. Among his crusades was a campaign to outlaw the horrible Indian practice of burning living widows on their husband's funeral pyres.

Roy was on a brief visit to Bristol in 1833 to meet friends and sympathisers including Miss Catherine Castle. He stayed at her home, Beech House in Stapleton which later became part of Purdown hospital.

Many of his visitors were women, for the impressive, handsome six foot tall aristocrat was celebrated in Europe for his calls for women's rights. He was also one of the first high caste Indians to visit Britain and so quite a star at the time.

Tragically, just 11 days after arriving in Bristol, he fell ill. Meningitis was diagnosed and he died soon afterwards.

Roy was first buried in the garden of Beech House but, 10 years later, his remains were moved to Arno's Vale and the monument commissioned by his disciple Dvarkanath Tagore built over his grave.

The monument is, incidentally, the only piece of true Hindu architecture in Britain.

The medieval treasure Bristol gave away

The Bristol Cross is one of the smaller architectural treasures of Britain – but it's one which Bristol's worthies were only too glad to give away.

Today the Cross has pride of place at Stourhead, the world-famous 18th century pleasure gardens which the banker Henry Hoare built near Mere in Wiltshire.

This medieval masterpiece was set up in Bristol in 1373 and it stood on High Street with its statues of four kings of England. More than two centuries later, in 1633, the figures of a further four monarchs were added, including one of Good Queen Bess, Elizabeth I, who had made such an impact during her visit to Bristol in 1574.

But Bristol's civic leaders declared this lovely monument an unsafe nuisance in its position on one of the city's busiest roads and in 1733 it was dismantled and moved to College Green where, if it fell down, it was less likely to hurt anyone.

Thirty years later the Cross was dismantled once again and this time its stones were piled into a corner of Bristol Cathedral for some later use. The heap of old masonry was a constant irritation to the cathedral staff and when the romantic Mr Hoare agreed to add it to his collection of follies at Stourhead, Bristol's leaders were delighted.

It has stayed at Stourhead ever since, a famous landmark at the entrance to one of the loveliest pleasure gardens in the world.

A truncated Victorian replica stands in Berkeley Square near the top of Park Street.

The oddest ball

Brunel's Ball is one of the oddest sights you'll find in and around Bristol University. It's a massive boulder which now stands on display on the university's big lawn alongside Woodland Road.

This huge spherical rock was one of two big natural nodules dug out in 1837 during the digging of the Great Western Railway tunnel at St Anne's. Brunel was so delighted with them that he had the pair mounted on pedestals at the eastern end of the tunnel.

Legend has it that the university's ball fell into the path of an express train half a century later and it was only thanks to the bravery of quarryman John Chiddy, who was killed clearing it off the line, that a major tragedy was averted.

But there is no doubt that in the 1980s British Rail, concerned at the ball's deterioration because of the damage being caused by the rumbling of passing trains, offered the memento to the university for safe-keeping.

Brunel's Ball is clearly visible from Woodland Road . . . but its plaque bears no mention of John Chiddy. Bristol University had hoped to credit the Victorian hero, but British Rail has no record to support his tale of heroism.

Whitchurch - Britain's top glamour airport

Whitchurch - gateway to the world for film stars, world leaders, Royalty, ambassadors and generals.

Hard to believe? Well, it's all true.

Whitchurch today is a quiet south Bristol suburb with a rather large open space in its midst . . . the windswept remains of Whitchurch Aerodrome. The tarmac runways are pitted, the place is deserted but in World War II this was a scene of hustle and bustle during Whitchurch's moment of glory as Great Britain's only civil airport with links to the outside world.

When war was declared in 1939, the great Imperial Airways and British Airways fleets of airliners were hurried down from London to Bristol for safety.

Two years later a daily service from Bristol to Lisbon, capital of neutral Portugal was established. It was the only civil flight out of Britain and pilots had to brave the occasional Luftwaffe attacks on the leg across the Bay of Biscay, which lay within easy range of enemy-occupied France. Usually an uneasy, unwritten truce protected the Bristol-based airliners.

The greatest, grandest and most famous used the Whitchurch-Lisbon route as their passage to the Portuguese staging post to a world beyond beleaguered Britain and occupied Europe.

Just one aircraft was lost on the journey. Typically, it carried several VIPs, the best-known the film star Leslie Howard.

Whitchurch aerodrome's glory faded quickly. The war over, the great airliners were back in London and in 1957 Bristol opened its new airport at Lulsgate.

The great Bedminster zeppelin raid myth

The myth has lingered for years . . . that Bedminster suffered a raid by a German airship during the First World War. The tale is still told . . . and there isn't a word of truth in it.

Memory plays curious tricks and the Bedminster airship raid is a particularly potent example.

Bristol certainly did take air raid precautions against zeppelin attacks in the 1914-18 war - churches were banned from ringing bells for fear they might act as sound beacons to an approaching fleet of enemy airships and a blackout was imposed - but the city's airspace was never invaded, even though Bristol was a leading manufacturer of planes, poison gas, explosives and weapons.

So how did this curious legend arise?

Almost certainly because Bedminster really was overflown by the *Graf Zeppelin* piloted by the great airship pioneer Hugo Eckener - not as an enemy but as guest on a courtesy flight over Bristol on July 7 1932, part of a whirlwind 24 hour tour of Britain.

Eckener and his crew flew over Filton, the Gloucester Road, the Centre, Whiteladies Road, the Avon Gorge and Bedminster and Ashton before heading towards Weston-super-Mare and Wales.

The *Graf Zeppelin*'s sensational appearance over Bedminster was followed, nine years later, by appalling bomb damage in the area. The events became confused in local memory, people recalled zeppelin raids on London during the First World War . . . and so grew the myth of the Bedminster airship blitz.

Shipshape and Bristol Fashion

Everyone knows this famous old expression about Bristol in its heyday as one of the world's greatest ports – and almost everyone gets it wrong when explaining what the saying really means.

No, it does not, as most people think, serve as a compliment to the tidiness of yesterday's seafaring Bristol and the smartness of its ocean-going vessels, their rigging and their well turned out crews.

Instead this expression dates back to a time when the City Docks were tidal with a very nasty rise and fall of water which left ships stranded on sharp mudbanks when the level was low and which had their timber hulls groaning with the strain each tide brought.

Any ship which fetched up in the port of Bristol needed a good, stout frame to withstand the sort of pressures a few days moored in Bristol involved.

If your boat wasn't Shipshape and Bristol Fashion, then it was best to sail well clear of the old port. The alternative was a very expensive delay for repairs!

Left *'Shipshape and Bristol Fashion': the city centre before it was covered over*

More Books about Bristol

Redcliffe have now published 100 books about Bristol. If you've enjoyed Offbeat Bristol we're sure you'll like many of our other local interest books. Here are just a few ideas.

Bristol & Co. by Helen Reid £4.95
A history of old established Bristol firms – from butchers to stockbrokers.

Bristol Between the Wars by David Harrison £4.95
Bristol seen through the eyes of those who lived through two decades of change, richly illustrated with contemporary photographs.

Bristol Blitz: The Untold Story by Helen Reid £3.95
A picture of Bristol and its people at war, with many photographs never before printed because of wartime censorship.

Bristol in the Fifties edited by James Belsey £4.95
Bristol's best writers recall life in Bristol as it was 30 to 40 years ago.

Famous Bristolians by David Foot £1.25
An illustrated alphabet of Bristol personalities.

Images of Bristol by James Belsey & David Harrison £5.95
A selection of Victorian and Edwardian photographs showing life in Bristol in the nineteenth century.

The Story of Bristol: from Middle Ages to Today by Bryan Little £6.95
A concise account of Bristol's fascinating, sometimes turbulent, history.

You should find these in any Bristol bookshop but if you have any problems they are obtainable direct from us at 49 Park Street, Bristol 1. Why not ask for our full catalogue?